T0143950

FROM THE AUTHOR OF
"THE AUDACITY OF VERACITY"

DARE TO
Live Life
FEARLESSLY

SPENDING LESS TIME IN
DIGITAL WORLD AND MORE
IN REAL WORLD

NICKY DARE

DAREinspires SERIES

Dare to Live Life Fearlessly

Copyright © 2020 by NICKY DARE.

All rights reserved. No part of this book may be reproduced or transmitted in any form or by any means, electronic or mechanical, including photocopying, recording, or by any information storage and retrieval system, without permission in writing from the copyright owner.

To order additional copies of this book, contact:
Xlibris
1-888-795-4274
www.Xlibris.com
Orders@Xlibris.com

For information contact:
www.NickyDare.com
Education.NickyDare.com

Books are available on paperback and kindle, on Amazon and other participating stores.

ISBN: 978-1-9845-7891-4 (sc)
ISBN: 978-1-9845-7892-1 (e)

Print information available on the last page

Rev. date: 05/27/2020

TABLE OF CONTENTS

"The state of my condition is uncertain… so I wait, pray, and continue to live according to the dictates of iDARE*. I get out, breathe, and enjoy nature's countless gifts.

One thing is certain: … a future of hope and love, inhering with the freedom to make a life of my own choosing and to share with everyone – and with you."

Nicky Dare "The Audacity of Veracity" page 176

*iDARE is an acronym for integrity, Diversity, Adaptation, Resilience, Empowerment.

Disclaimer

This book has been written for information purposes only. Every effort has been made to make this book as complete and accurate as possible. However, there may be mistakes in typography or content. Also, this book provides information only up to the publishing date. Therefore, this book should be used as a guide - not as the ultimate source.

The purpose of this book is to **educate**. The author and the publisher do not warrant that the information contained in this e-book is fully complete and shall not be responsible for any errors or omissions. The author and publisher shall have neither liability nor responsibility to any person or entity with respect to any loss or damage caused or alleged to be caused directly or indirectly by this book.

About the Author

Live and Love Fearlessly!

"I believe that knowledge is power. Everyone should improve themselves and/or business, no matter what stage in life they're in. Without obstacles, we never would know the true meaning of success or feel the exaltation of triumph over adversity. Mindset is the anchor to your resilience. Moving forward is key. Live and Love Fearlessly!"

Ms. Dare is an outdoor enthusiast whose life journey has been part of fulfilling her personal development. In the past decades, Dare spent most of her lifetime enjoying the outdoors, experiencing the survival wilderness, as well as learning urban survival challenges in different parts of the world. She uses her real-world insights to help educate and train many people and organizations. If you would like to learn more from Nicky Dare, please visit:

www.NickyDare.com

To My Father

You Were The Ultimate Mentor

I Miss You Everyday

To My Mother,

The Bedrock of My Life,

My CaveMan and My Pumkin,

The Safeguards of My World,

You Mean The World To Me

Dihatiku Selalu

DARE To Live Life

INTRODUCTION

Introduction

It is becoming very challenging to put the phone down. Not only are most people working in front of a screen all day, but most do it at home too (speaking from the experience myself). Several people go home after work and sit in front of the TV and browse their phone.

We live a digitalized life. Over 80% of the population owns a mobile device, and 57% of them have more than one type of device. Not only are our electronic devices connected to the internet, but it is also in our car, the fridge, our watch, our games, and even our home. This omnipresence of technology begs the question, how can we free ourselves from an addiction to the digital world?

Here's a short survey that will give you an idea of your relationship with technology. While this is not a scientific survey, it gives you an idea of your relationship with the digital world.

	YES	NO	I DON'T KNOW
Do you sleep with your phone next to your bed?			
Do you look at social media an hour or less before bed?			
Is it hard for you to sit in silence (ex: on your commute or in a car)?			
Do you eat most of your meals in front of a screen?			
Do you use your phone as an alarm?			
Do you check social media while you are at work?			
Do you usually check your phone as soon as there is a notification?			
Do you turn on the TV when you come home from work?			
Do you have a smartwatch?			
Would you say that your daily screen time is more than 5 hours a day?			
Is looking at your phone an automatic behavior that you don't always do consciously?			
Do you have a hard time falling asleep or staying asleep?			
Do you struggle with weight?			

	YES	NO	I DON'T KNOW
Do you have difficulty with your attention or concentration?			
Do you check your phone or browse social media when you drive?			
Do you sometimes feel like your phone vibrate, and yet there are no notifications?			
Do you feel anxious if you forget your phone or don't have access to it for a while?			
Does it irritate you when people tell you that you are not listening or paying attention to them while they speak to you?			
Would you consider your electronic devices as your most valuable belongings, something you could not live without?			
TOTALS			
	YES	**NO**	**I DON'T KNOW**

Now calculate the totals, what do you notice?

Mostly NO: Great, that means that you have found a spot in your life where you use devices and, they don't use you and admittedly don't govern your life. Yes, this includes the restrooms!

Mostly YES: This is a sign that this guide is for you. Your life seems to be influenced a lot by your screen time; you might be losing a lot of time and energy on devices that don't fulfill you. Besides, if you said "yes" to almost all the questions, you are likely an artist at escaping reality. It might be time for you to take control of your life. It won't be easy to unplug, but with determination and patience, you will get there!

Mostly I DON'T KNOW: This is not necessarily a good thing. You might be in denial and unable to be aware of your behavior. This guide will help you be more conscious of your habits and how you can live a more fulfilling life.

Whether you want to completely break up with social media or develop a healthier relationship with technology, this guide is here to help you positively change your behaviors. This guide will help you reconnect with your life. After reading this book, you will be able to recognize the actions that affect your physical and mental health and learn how you can adopt more effective habits to be happier.

You will learn about the current state of the digital world, what the impact is on your physical and mental health. We will explore how you can adopt more positive behaviors with technology while finding a way to reconnect with yourself. The last part of this guide is a 21-day plan that will help you break up with technology for good. But first, let's look at what history is and the current state of our digital life.

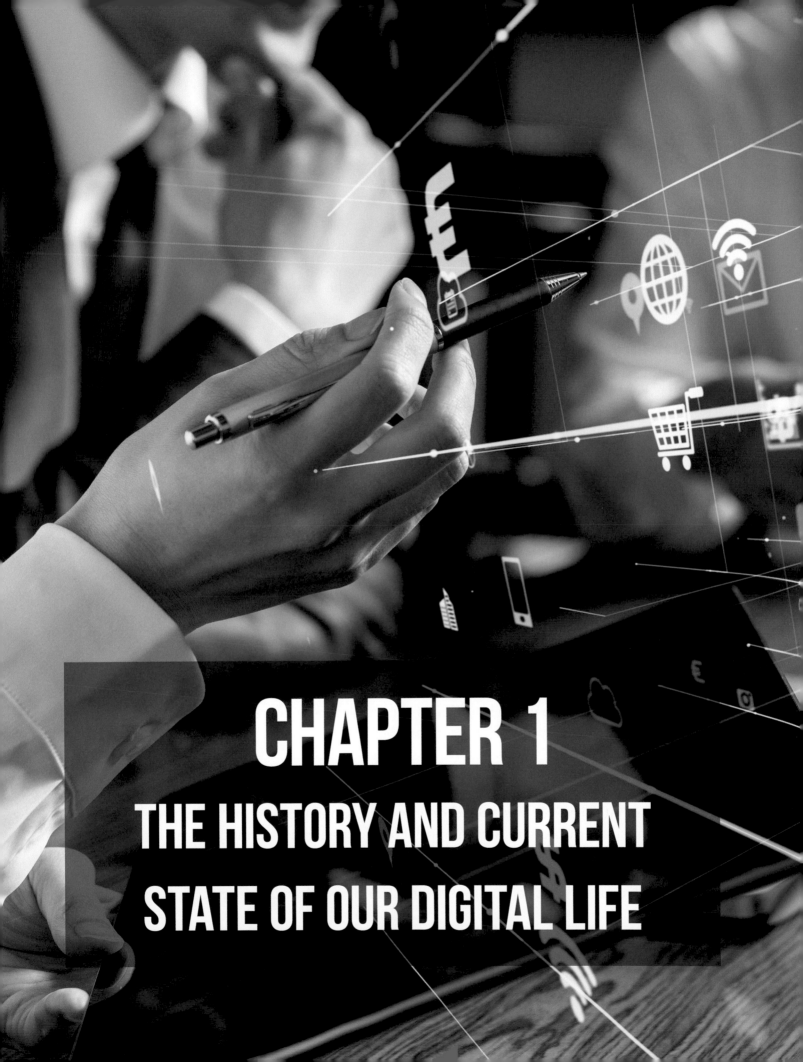

CHAPTER 1
THE HISTORY AND CURRENT STATE OF OUR DIGITAL LIFE

Chapter 1: The History and Current State of Our Digital Life

Technology has been changing our lives for years, but it hasn't always been for the best. There is a fantastic advancement in the area of health care where people can walk again or communicate with the assistance of technology. On the other hand, technology can also limit us, especially when we become addicted to it.

The History

While the phone was patented in the 1870s, it moved from being a landline to mobile later in history. It is hard to believe that the handheld mobile phone was mass-produced less than 50 years ago, in 1973. So much has changed since. Texting came about 20 years later (1992), and the iPhone was launched in 2007. With its mass presence, it is so easy to forget how life was before the smartphone.

Another technology that is relatively young in history is the internet. The internet became public on August 6, 1991, less than 30 years ago. It has been with us ever since, improving its speed every year and no longer just accessible on computers.

The Current State

It doesn't matter where you live in the world; screen time is becoming a global issue. Over 45% of the world population has a smartphone (which is around 3.5 billion people); this is more than a 30% increase since 2016.

The screen time worldwide is, on average, 6h42min, with no significant difference between gender. In research done in the UK, 99% of children between the ages of 12–15 are online and have an average screen time of 21 hours per week.

While the World Health Organization (WHO) provided some guidelines for screen time and children, there are no guidelines that exist for adults. It is up to us to decide what we believe is an appropriate time we can spend online. It is probably only a matter of time before the government starts publishing recommendations for health concerning screen time.

The next chapters will provide you with more knowledge about the health impact. These chapters will focus on physical and mental health and how it can be affected by our screen time.

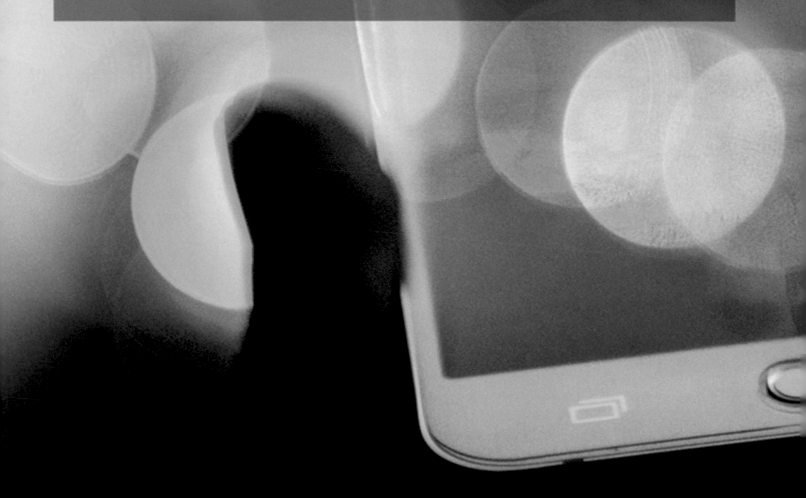

CHAPTER 2
THE DIGITAL IMPACT
ON YOUR BODY

Chapter 2: The Digital Impact on Your Body

A group of studies is starting to demonstrate the impact of technology on our bodies. It is safe to say that we are very limited in the knowledge and research about the long-term effects of technology. As people age with social media and wireless technology, we will likely have more discoveries that change our relationship with the digital world. For now, here are a few known issues.

Obesity

Unsurprisingly, obesity, and screen time are connected. A large study of over 90,000 participants concluded that independent of physical activity, it was observed that obesity and screen time are positively correlated. A longitudinal study showed that 60% of overweight incidence in their study was attributable to excess television viewing.

Vision

Another impact on our physical health is our vision. A growing body of research indicates that around 50% of the population will experience Digital Eye Strain (DES). DES is a syndrome that causes a person to have various symptoms like sore, dried, tired, burning or itching eyes, headaches, sore neck, or even a difficulty keeping your eyes open. It can undoubtedly be treated, but no studies demonstrate the long-term impact on our vision.

Posture

Screen time can also impact your posture. A study by Harvard, Brigham and Women's Hospital, and Microsoft show that spending too much time on small devices like a phone can strain muscles, nerves, tendons, ligaments, and spinal discs.

Sleep

Finally, one of the most prevalent physical health impacts of too much screen time is the lack of quality sleep. Research has now demonstrated that the screen light (called blue light) of our device can stimulate the cells in our eyes and reset our internal clock, which is the circadian rhythm. Not only does this affect our sleep, but it could also cause some health issues since circadian rhythm issues are connected to cancer, metabolism issues, and cognitive dysfunctions.

Since sleep is a big challenge for many people, the next chapter will provide you with tips on how you can improve your bedtime routine and get more sleep every night.

CHAPTER 3
LEARN TO SLEEP AGAIN

Chapter 3: Learn to Sleep Again

Speaking from years of hands-on experience, I know this too well and close to my heart. As a result of increased screen time, the body tends to delay the production of melatonin, a vital hormone that regulates our sleep. Over time, that sleep deprivation can lead to something more severe, like mood disorders, obesity, or depression.

To improve your nights of sleep, here are recommendations that you can implement in your bedtime routine to increase your chance of good night sleep. Please take good care of your body, mind, and overall health. After all, only you know what is best for you!

Create a Schedule

It is proven that a routine will trick your body into falling asleep at a specific time. Try to observe yourself, is there a time when you are tired? If so, make sure you go to bed before that time. Create a routine that allows you to complete everything before that time and go to bed. You can also set an alarm that will tell you that it's time to prepare yourself for bedtime. That way, you are less likely going to forget what time it is and be more successful at implementing a routine.

Create a Ritual

A bedtime ritual is an excellent addition to your schedule. A good bedtime ritual is one that allows you to relax, disconnect from the stress of life, and slowly tell your body that it is time to shut down. Here are a few things you can add to your ritual:

- Take a bath
- Go to bed 1 hour before bedtime and read a book (but not a too engaging book)
- Drink an herbal tea
- Listen to calming music
- Write in a journal
- Do a meditation

During that hour before bed, it is essential to avoid bright light; that way, you don't reset your circadian rhythm. A small tip: I use one of those girlie eye covers to go to bed. It does help me sleep nicely.

Create a Comfortable Atmosphere

Don't' underestimate the comfort of your bed and pillow and the power of fresh linen. If you are uncomfortable, you will likely have a hard time falling asleep or staying asleep. Another aspect of comfort is the temperature of the room and the level of noise around. Try sleeping with a fan on or a white noise machine. Having a constant sound in the room could help you maintain your sleep. If you like essential oils, try a drop of lavender on your pillow, this will help the brain relax. Personally, I highly recommend eucalyptus oil – but then, I absolutely love all scents of any essential oils.

Avoid Certain Foods or Substances

Avoid any alcohol, cigarettes, caffeine, or a large meal from 2–3 hours before you go to bed.

Turn Off Your Devices

This will probably be the most challenging thing to do but the most impactful, which is to turn off any electronics 1 hour before bedtime. Spend the last hour doing something calming and relaxing. Try to have your device outside the bedroom during the night; this will allow you not to be disturbed during your sleep. Experts say that the bed should be used for sleep and sex. If you work, browse social media or watch TV from your bed, your brain will associate the bed with a zone of activity and will likely be active even when it is bedtime. Train your mind to see your bed as a place to disconnect from the digital world.

Room Make-Over

It might be time to look at your bedroom and try to find ways to improve the atmosphere for a good night's sleep. Are there electronics that make it bright at night, like the light on a laptop charger or your alarm clock? Make sure that you can remove the light and make the space dark for sleep. Also, consider moving the TV in your bedroom. The TV will stimulate you instead of encouraging sleep.

Talk to an Expert

If you've tried all those recommendations and you are still struggling with sleep, it might be a good idea to consult your doctor or a sleep expert. There are other solutions that they can provide you with to improve your sleep situation.

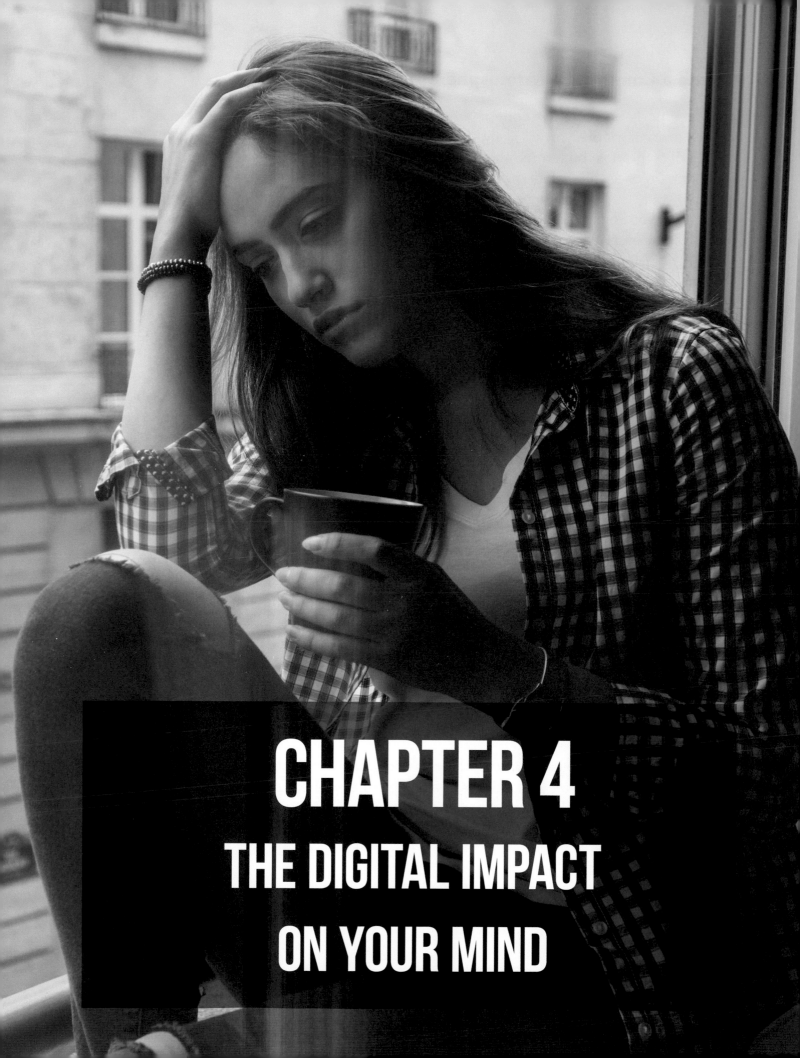

CHAPTER 4
THE DIGITAL IMPACT
ON YOUR MIND

Chapter 4: The Digital Impact on Your Mind

Now that we've covered the impact of our electronic devices on the physical body let's look at its effects on the mental body. The technology has made such a significant impact on our psyche that we now have new terms that describe psychological issues such as FOMO.

FOMO, or Fear of Missing Out, is described as "anxiety that an exciting or interesting event may currently be happening elsewhere, often aroused by posts seen on a social media website." Not only will we experience real symptoms caused by social media, but the mind will also create false reactions like "phantom vibration syndrome." Which is when you feel your phone vibrating, but it didn't.

Studies show that the new generations are now dreaming in color and therefore demonstrate how much technology can impact the mind. Dreaming in color is a unique occurrence connected to generations of individuals who grew up with colored TV screens.

Let's dig a bit deeper into how the digital world impacts our minds.

Dopamine: The Feel-Good Hormone

The most astonishing finding of the impact of technology on our behavior and mind is how it stimulates the dopamine. Dopamine is a neurotransmitter that is responsible for pleasure, desire, ambition, addiction, and sex drive. Research now shows that social media users experience a similar dopamine cycle as individuals who are addicted to alcohol, cigarettes, and drugs.

Anxiety

In a study by Cheever and colleagues (2014), two groups were studies. One group was allowed to have their phone but had to shut it down during the research. The other group had to give up their phone for the duration of the study. The results show that anxiety levels rose over time, not only in the group that didn't have access to their phone but also amongst heavy smartphone users that were in the other group. The anxiety that arises from smartphone utilization can be associated with our Fear of Missing out (FOMO).

FOMO: Fear of Missing Out

FOMO is a feeling of anxiety that experienced we think we are missing out on something. It is a collective term that we see in connection with social media use or online shopping. Based on surveys, 56% of social media users experience FOMO, and 69% of the millennials will experience it daily. Many kinds of research now demonstrate that FOMO is connected to the overuse of smartphones and smartphone addiction, which impacts around 50% of young adults.

Phantom Vibration Syndrome

As mentioned before, phantom vibration syndrome it the perceived vibrations from a device that is not vibrating. In research done with over 250 undergraduates, 89% had experienced phantom vibration.

Depression

Several studies now demonstrate that individuals who spend more time on social media have higher rates of depression than those who spend less time. There's also a link with suicide risk factors where teens who spend 5 hours or more on their phone are 71% more likely to exhibit those factors. Besides, the suicide rate increase in teenagers seems to correlate with the phone usage increase between the years 2007–2015.

Attention

One of the most prominent displayed impacts of our digital world is the lack of focus and awareness. The attention span in our digital world has gone from 12 seconds in 2000 to 8 seconds today 2015 (this is less than a goldfish's attention, which is about 9 seconds). This lack of awareness has a significant impact on our daily life. For example, the average user will lose over 3 hours a week just by picking up their phone. Our lack of attention makes us more forgetful, less engage with others, and also exhausted. According to some studies, this constant distraction can lead us to be 40% less productive during our day.

Since the lack of attention seems to be prevalent in most of us, the next chapter will provide you with ideas to improve your awareness and concentration during your day.

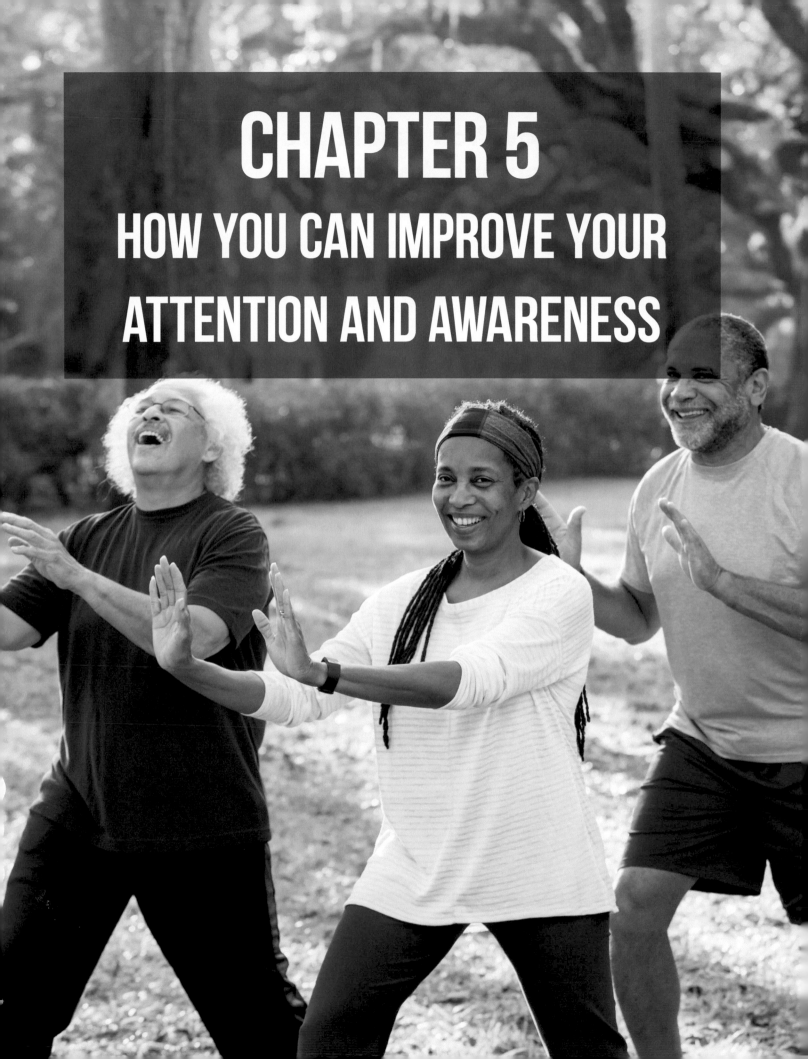

CHAPTER 5
HOW YOU CAN IMPROVE YOUR ATTENTION AND AWARENESS

Chapter 5: How You Can Improve Your Attention and Awareness

To improve your attention, you need to increase your ability to bring yourself in the present moment. Practicing awareness can be done in a way that it is part of your daily routine. You will need to be disciplined, which means that you have to carve time in your day when you can practice. Here are a few things you can do:

Exercise

Exercises like yoga or running can be a great way to practice being in the present moment. Research shows that when you exercise, you are more likely to increase the control of your mind. Exercising is also connected with increased attention in school and academic scores.

Meditate

Meditation is practicing awareness. Many people believe that they have to stop thinking when they meditate. Yet, meditation is not about stopping yourself from doing something; it is more about observing what is happening within you and around you. A simple way to meditate is to sit down and focus on a sound in the room. That sound can be a fan or a refrigerator. When you catch yourself drifting from that focus, bring your awareness back to the sound. You can do that for 15 minutes at a time daily. The goal is to observe yourself drifting and go back to the task.

Read

Reading is a great way to increase your ability to focus and pay attention to one task at a time. If you are reading on your mobile device, make sure to turn off all notifications so that you are not distracted during your reading. A great time to read is before bed, as it allows you to disconnect from the digital world and also calm your mind before going to sleep. It is preferable to use a book, which doesn't stimulate the brain as a screen would. Your local library likely has excellent books for you!

Write in a Journal

Journaling is another activity that can be done before bed and is a great way to focus your thoughts on one thing. Nowadays, there are useful journals that encourage thinking, or you can go simple and get a notebook and write your day in it or make it a grateful journal.

I have started journaling since I can remember myself writing as a young girl. In fact, I believe my mother still keeps my original journal diary from my years in high school and college. In it, I would write about my dreams, my vision, what I want to achieve in my life. Writing down your thoughts has been an outlet for me, a positive 'get away' more than just a 'wish list' or goal setting white board. It's more than just writing down your thoughts and feelings so that you can understand them more clearly. Keeping a journal or diary may help tremendously when you struggle with stress, depression, anxiety. It can help you gain control of your own emotions and improve your brain health.

Make a List

How many times have you found yourself distracted from work because you had a sudden question in your head that lead you to browse Google for 15 minutes? It is so easy to be distracted when you give energy to every thought you have. Instead of acting on every idea, make a list. Keep a pen and paper close and when you have a thought like, what is a good recipe for chicken or what is the weather tomorrow, write it down. The list will be an excellent way to put your thoughts down without distracting you for too long. When you need a pause from work, look at your list.

CHAPTER 6
HOW THE DIGITAL WORLD IS SHAPING YOUR BEHAVIOR

Chapter 6: How the Digital World Is Shaping Your Behavior

As you have seen from the impact of the digital world on our mind and physical body, we are gravely influenced by our screen time. This influence can also shape our behavior.

We often hear that technology is something that can change our behaviors for the best; for example, the use of smartwatch to increase exercises or games like Pokémon Go to get children outside. But is this positive behavior change a reality?

It is a known fact that marketing firms and media study psychology to shape the behaviors of their users. You have probably noticed that the use of shocking titles or the sound notification of social media is very good at grabbing your attention. These tactics are shaping human interactions and behaviors. Nowadays, people are more likely to interrupt a conversation with another individual if their smartwatch or phone vibrates. This behavior can be extremely irritating for the person on the other side of the conversation.

We are consistently entertained and receive instant gratification by our electronics. It's almost like solitude or silence has become taboo or worse, feared. Just ask yourself when the last time you sat in silence? Are you able to drive from point A. to point B. without music? Besides, we don't tolerate waiting anymore. People are getting more short-tempered on the roads and in line at the café.

Another behavior is our constant need for attention from others with selfies and likes. This attention-seeking culture is making us create this "cyber self" that is often our perceived perfect self and world. It is a world where we can use filters to hide some inconsistencies on our skin or make our face narrower to be more pleasing. Selfies have a particular objective, which is to determine if others like it or not. This world of selfies has led to another type of behavior, which is to dress for Instagram. Some people's world becomes driven by their digital self.

Being distracted by our devices all the time is making us uncomfortable with being alone with ourselves. It can also make us less capable of dealing with our thoughts and emotions. When we lose track of our true selves and become obsessed with what the external world thinks of us, we become easily manipulated and influenced by others. We lose the ability to think for ourselves and be independent.

Since our behavior is connected to our emotions, our screen time is likely going to influence how we feel. In the next chapter, we will learn about emotional awareness and how you can better control your emotions in the digital world.

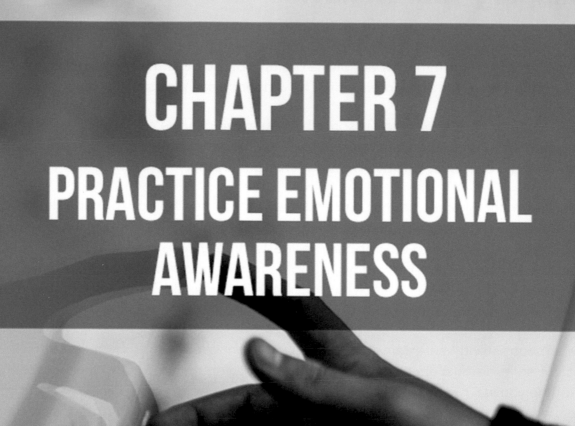

CHAPTER 7
PRACTICE EMOTIONAL AWARENESS

Chapter 7: Practice Emotional Awareness

When we are consistently entertained by something external to us, it is easy to let our feelings and emotions be in sync with what we are watching on the screen. Whether you are looking at selfies or watching a horrible video, your emotional state will be influenced and likely create some emotional turmoil that is avoidable.

Some research has concluded that social media lead, in general, toward negative emotions. For example, a study demonstrated that Facebook users had an elevated feeling of envy. While limiting the usage of social media is the best recommendation; being aware of how social media is affecting you is very important if you want to improve your emotional state.

Here are a few suggestions on how you can do this:

Next time you are on social media, observe your emotional state. Every time you experience a negative emotional state, make a mental note of it.

When you observe yourself feeling negative emotions, shift your mind to something more positive or put your phone down for a minute.

If you find yourself triggered by a post, unfollow that person. Clean your Social Media and only follow individuals who make you feel good about yourself.

The key is to be an emotion aware user and know when to quit. The more you will practice observation of yourself when you are online, the better you will become at avoiding situations that put you in a reactive state as opposed to a reflective mode. When you catch yourself going down that reactive mode, shift your attention to something more empowering.

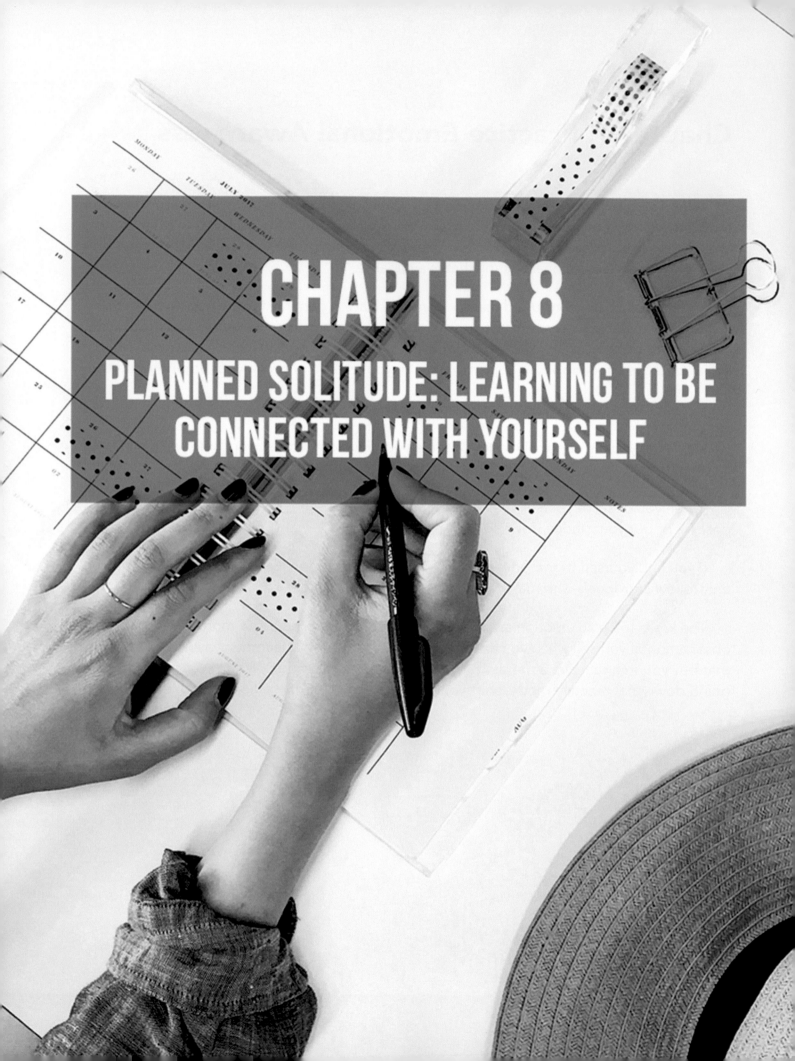

CHAPTER 8

PLANNED SOLITUDE: LEARNING TO BE CONNECTED WITH YOURSELF

Chapter 8: Planned Solitude: Learning to Be Connected With Yourself

A great way to disconnect with the digital world is to set a time when you will make the "unplugging" official. You can do so by planning a time of solitude.

In the world of psychology, solitude is known to improve psychological well-being; it helps you get to know yourself and also allows you not to feel lonely when unplanned solitude happens.

It can be seen as a reset button where you can go back to what drives you and also be inspired to be your best self. Planned solitude doesn't have to be for a long time or boring. Here are a few things you can do to get more familiar with being alone and comfortable in silence.

Go for a Ride

Ride a car, a bike, or even a motorcycle! During that hour, do not bring any electronic devices, and if you are in a car, turn off the radio. During that time, you will enjoy your own company and the sounds around you.

Go to a Local Café

A local café is an excellent location if you want to be alone but not entirely isolated. Leave your phone at home or in the car. Grab a cup of your favorite java and sit down alone. Observe what is around you, practice mindfulness, which is to listen, observe, and live in the present moment.

Go for a Walk

Search for a trail in your area and go for a hike! Leave your music and devices in the car or at home. Take this opportunity to connect with nature, get some fresh air, and empty your mind.

Go to a Retreat

Why not plan a weekend retreat or a night away from home? Try to find a place where you can be close to nature and reconnect with yourself. It doesn't have to be an expensive getaway; it can be a home vacation rental a few miles away from you. Try not to bring your electronic devices and completely disconnect for 24 hours.

Planned solitude is only one way to unplug from the digital world. In the next chapter, you will learn other options that are available to you when it comes to reconnecting with your reality.

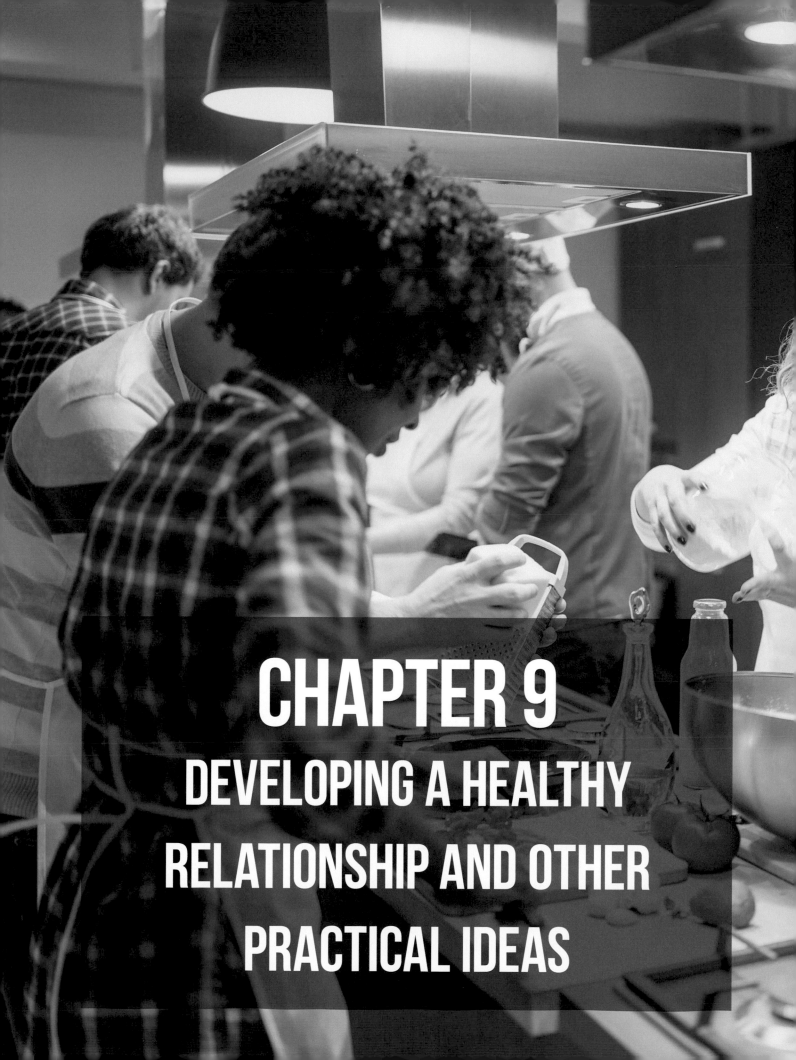

CHAPTER 9
DEVELOPING A HEALTHY RELATIONSHIP AND OTHER PRACTICAL IDEAS

Chapter 9: Developing a Healthy Relationship and Other Practical Ideas

There are many ways to unplug with the digital world. You've already seen a few in the chapters above. To be successful, you have to identify as many activities that do not require a screen. Make sure to pick something that appeals to you and won't be challenging to do. Here are a few options you might want to try.

Tech-Free Rooms

Choose a room or rooms in your home where electronics are not welcomed. It could be a spare room that you transform into a meditation room or remove all electronics from your bedroom. That zone will be an excellent place to go when you want to unplug.

Unplug Time

Have a time range when you choose to unplug. That could be in the morning before going to work, during meals or an hour before bed. Dedicate that time to activities that don't require you to be in front of a screen. Also, you can choose a whole day instead of a time range. A bit like Meatless Monday, you could have a Tech-Free Tuesday.

Let It Die

Another way to avoid always being on your electronic device is to let it die. When your phone or smartwatch dies, take it as a sign that you need to take some offline time. Avoid looking at your device while it charges by turning it off. Place it on the charge and do an activity that is not in front of a screen.

Take a Class

Why not enroll in a local course? That way, you will spend your time learning something new with other people instead of wasting your time on social media. Local colleges usually offer evening or weekend classes to the general public. There is a wide variety of options available to you, such as learning a new art, a foreign language, new recipes, or even an exercise class like kickboxing or dance.

Join a Club

Are you interested in bowling or reading? Or maybe you are more a food or wine tasting type of person? Whatever your interest is, you can indeed find a group of people in your area that have similar interests as you. By joining a club, you will have less need to be on social media and have more success in your social life.

Boardgame Night

Start your own "unplug" evening by inviting friends over for a game night. Board games are always an excellent option when you want to have fun with friends.

Ignore Notifications

Train yourself to ignore your phone notifications. Just like Pavlov's research with a dog's response to a stimulus, you are currently trained to respond immediately to a notification alarm on your phone. It's time for you to retrain yourself. From now on, you can use the notification of your smart device as a reminder to breathe. Every time a notification sound arises, take a deep breath through the nose and exhale through the mouth. You can also use this opportunity to compliment yourself or make it a moment of gratitude. The more often you will practice this new behavior, the quicker it will become a habit.

The more you are distracted from grabbing your phone or sitting in front of the TV, the easier it will be for you to disconnect.

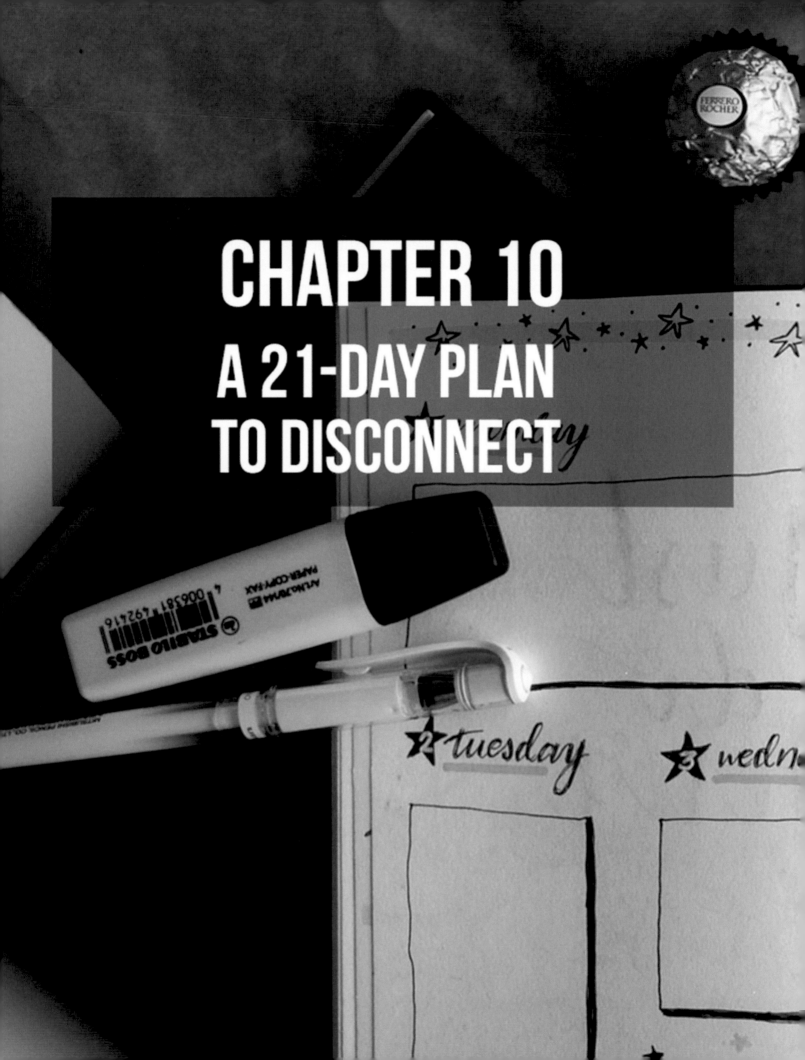

CHAPTER 10
A 21-DAY PLAN TO DISCONNECT

Chapter 10: A 21-Day Plan to Disconnect for Good

The following plan is to help you develop a healthier relationship with the digital world. You will be slowly guided to reduce your screen time over 21 days. If you work in front of a screen, try to apply the following guidelines in your personal life.

Before you start this plan, ask yourself how ready you are to make that change. Your motivation to change will be the number one reason if you fail or not. Answer the following questions to assess your change readiness.

On a scale of 1 to 10 (1 being not motivated, 10 being highly motivated), how motivated are you to disconnect from the digital world?

1   2   3   4   5   6   7   8   9   10

If your answer was below 10, what would help you move one score higher? In other words, what would make you more motivated to change?

_____

What do you perceive as a benefit to disconnect?

_____

Who are the people that can help you with your goal? And how can you involve them?

_____

Preparation

To set yourself up for success, identify a time when you want to start. Make sure that you have conducive conditions for 21 days.

My start date will be: _____

Now that you have a start date hold yourself accountable and make sure to mark it on your calendar. If you live with other people, try to get them to participate with you, the more, the merrier (or, the easier).

Organize your space so that it is easier for you to avoid screen time. If you have a TV in your bedroom, it could be a great idea to move it to another room, the less temptation, the better.

Now let try to prepare you for the obstacles by predicting your behaviors.

Which times of the day are you mostly in front of a screen?

_____

_____

_____

What are the things you would like to do to replace screen time?

Examples: Reading, bowling, exercising, cooking, walking, etc.

_____

_____

_____

What could be the biggest obstacles to your success?

_____

_____

_____

What are your options to prevent those obstacles from arising?

_____

_____

_____

Think of a day when you are disconnected from the digital world. What would it look like?

_____

_____

_____

Now get ready, it's time to officially disconnected from the digital world.

Day 1: Monitoring Screen Time

Today, you will monitor your screen time. You can download an app that will calculate that for your phone and make sure to take note of screen time on other devices like TV or computers.

Your goal will be to see a reduction in screen time for the 21 days. Every morning, you will indicate your screen time of the previous day and aim to reduce it.

Day 1—Screen-time: _____

Day 2: Planned Offline

Today, I need to aim for _____ minutes of screen time.

Today, you will plan offline time. Identify a time when you will turn off all your devices for 30 minutes. Once you've identified a time, decide what you will do during that time. Feel free to pick something that you wrote in the preparation section.

At _____ am/pm, I will turn off my devices. I will keep myself occupied by doing _____.

Once you've completed your offline time, answer the following questions.

How did you feel during the planned offline?

_____

_____

_____

On a scale of 1 to 10 (1 being extremely difficult, 10 being extremely easy), how easy was it to spend 30 minutes without looking at a screen?

1   2   3   4   5   6   7   8   9   10

If your answer was below 10, what can you do next time to improve that score? Could you repeat the activity for a more extended period? __

_____

_____

_____

Today's screen-time result: _____ minutes

Day 3: Emotional Awareness

Today, I need to aim for _____ minutes of screen time.

Today, you will practice emotional awareness. Pay attention to your emotions while looking at a screen. Every time you catch yourself feeling down, take a timeout of one minute. During that minute, focus on your breathing. Take six deep breaths every time you have a negative emotion.

What else than breathing could you do to occupy that 1 minute?

Examples: Go for a quick walk around the house; Do a house chore; Get yourself a glass of water.

_____

_____

_____

How many timeouts did you take today? _____

What does it tell you about your emotions? What type of emotions did you notice (ex: sad, envy, anger, frustration, annoyance, etc.).

_____

_____

_____

How can you reduce the avoidable negative emotions you have in a day?

_____

_____

_____

Today's screen-time result: _____ minutes

Day 4: Planned Offline 2

Today, I need to aim for _____ minutes of screen time.

Today, you will plan two offline periods in your day. Allocate two 30 minutes today when you will turn off all your devices. Once you've identified a time, decide what you will do during these times.

At _____ am/pm, and _____ am/pm, I will turn off my devices. I will keep myself occupied by doing _____

_____

_____

Once you've completed your offline time, answer the following questions.

How did you feel during the planned offline times?

_____

_____

_____

On a scale of 1 to 10 (1 being extremely difficult, 10 being extremely easy), how easy was it to spend two 30 minutes without looking at a screen?

1   2   3   4   5   6   7   8   9   10

If your answer was below 10, what can you do next time to improve that score?

_____

_____

_____

Today's screen-time result: _____ minutes

Day 5: Charge Up

Today, I need to aim for _____ minutes of screen time.

Today, you will charge your smart devices outside of your bedroom during sleep time. If you use your phone as an alarm, you will need to find an alarm clock (not a smartwatch). You can also place your phone so that you can't access it during the night (example: on the other side of the room).

When you wake up tomorrow morning, do not look at your phone for 15–30 minutes after getting up. Switch your routine to make coffee, get ready for the day, or maybe take your shower first. Whatever you choose to do, be mindful of not looking at a screen for 15–30 minutes after getting out of bed.

Today's screen-time result: _____ minutes

Day 6: Get Some Fresh Air

Today, I need to aim for _____ minutes of screen time.

Today, you will leave your phone and smartwatch behind for 1 hour and get some fresh air. Chose to play mini-golf, cycle, or walk. Pick something that will occupy your mind for an hour. The more the activity is enjoyable for you, the less likely are you going to realize that you don't have your phone.

On a scale of 1 to 10 (1 being extremely difficult, 10 being extremely easy), how easy was it to spend 1 hour without your phone or smartwatch?

1   2   3   4   5   6   7   8   9   10

If your answer was below 10, what can you do next time to improve that score?

_____

_____

_____

Today's screen-time result: _____ minutes

Day 7: It's Your Choice!

Today, I need to aim for _____ minutes of screen time.

Today is the last day of the first week. How do you want to reconnect with your life today? Plan something that will allow you to turn off devices and experience reality.

_____

_____

_____

How do you feel after your first week?

_____

_____

_____

_____

What was easy? What are you proud of?

_____

_____

_____

_____

What was tricky? What could be done differently?

_____

_____

_____

_____

Today's screen-time result: _____ minutes

Day 8: Bedtime Routine

Today, I need to aim for _____ minutes of screen time.

You are now starting your second week. Congratulations!

Today, you will set a bedtime routine that doesn't include screen time. Thirty minutes to an hour before bed, you will turn off all devices and start a new bedtime routine. During that time, you can:

- Prepare your lunch for work tomorrow
- Read (not on electronics)
- Take a bath
- Write in a journal

- Make tea and drink it in silence
- Meditate
- Do stretches

Any other activity that doesn't require you to be in front of a screen and can help you relax.

Do your best to maintain that bedtime routine of no screen time 30 minutes to an hour before bed for the rest of the 21 days.

Today's screen-time result: _____ minutes

DAY 9: MINDFULNESS BREATHING

Today, I need to aim for _____ minutes of screen time.

In the next few days, you are going to explore the world of mindfulness.

For today, try mindfulness breathing by taking three deep breaths.

- Breathing in through the nose
- Breathing out through the mouth
- Repeat two more times

Redo this mindfulness breathing a few times during your day to make it a total of 5 mindfulness breathing activities.

Today's screen-time result: _____ minutes

Day 10: Mindfulness Eating

Today, I need to aim for _____ minutes of screen time.

Today, you will eat without your device and will bring your awareness to your eating. Every bite you take, place the utensils down on the table, and appreciate the taste of the food. It won't be easy at first, especially if you are hungry, but with practice, it becomes a habit.

How did you experience this activity?

_____

_____

_____

Today's screen-time result: _____ minutes

Day 11: Mindfulness Walking

Today, I need to aim for _____ minutes of screen time.

Today, you will pay attention to every step you take, slow down your pace, and feel your feet touching the ground. Observe how it feels to walk and also really focus on placing your heel, foot, and toes down on the ground for every step.

How does it feel to slow down the pace of your walk?

_____

_____

_____

Today's screen-time result: _____ minutes

Day 12: Mindfulness Browsing

Today, I need to aim for _____ minutes of screen time.

When you are browsing the internet today, pay attention to your feelings, and also try to be mindful of the speed of browsing. Try to read everything you see and complete the reading before moving on to something else. Observe yourself, how you react to certain things, and also try to stay focused on the task and not distracted by notifications.

How do you feel when you slow down your browsing speed?

_____

_____

_____

Today's screen-time result: _____ minutes

Day 13: Mindfulness Breathing 2

Today, I need to aim for _____ minutes of screen time.

Today you will practice the mindfulness breathing (taught earlier) every time you catch yourself looking at your electronic device.

- When you look at your phone or smartwatch, take three deep breaths before unlocking your device.

- Breathing in through the nose
- Breathing out through the mouth
- Repeat two more times
- Once you are done your breathing exercise, ask yourself if you really need to look at your phone or if you can go back to the task you were doing. Redo this mindfulness breathing every time you look at your device.

Did mindfulness breathing make a difference in your attention today?

_____

_____

_____

Today's screen-time result: _____ minutes

Day 14: Mindfulness Browsing 2

Today, I need to aim for _____ minutes of screen time.

Today, you will go on your social media account. For 20 minutes, you will look at every post on your feed and observe your feelings. Unfollow every user that posts something that doesn't bring you a positive experience.

This task will be an excellent clean-up and will improve your experience when you are on social media.

How many people did you unfollow?

_____

_____

_____

Today's screen-time result: _____ minutes

Day 15: Reflection

Today, I need to aim for _____ minutes of screen time.

You are starting the third week. Congratulations!

How do you feel so far?

_____

_____

_____

How would you like to start day 15? This is your last week, identify something that you want to do all week to help you unplug.

_____

_____

_____

Today's screen-time result: _____ minutes

Day 16: Unplug

Today, I need to aim for _____ minutes of screen time.

Today is the big day; you will turn off your devices for half the day (unless your work is in front of the screen, if that is the case, no personal browsing). Yes, you read that right. Turn off your devices now.

If you are starting to formulate an excuse in your mind for not turning off your devices, stop yourself right now. THERE ARE NO EXCUSES. If people need to reach you, give them your work phone number or office email. But there is absolutely no reason you can't turn off your phone for half a day (let's say 6 hours).

If you are still making up excuses in your mind, at least try it for one hour. After an hour, turn on your phone to see if you have any emergencies, and turn it off for another hour. There is no need to be on your phone for longer than 5 minutes. That should be plenty of time to check if somebody tried to reach you for an emergency. If you can't even do that, maybe ask a friend to help you with the activity. Your friend might also be open to hold your phone for you and let you know if something urgent comes up.

Today's screen-time result: _____ minutes

Day 17: 24 Hour Cleanse

Today, I need to aim for _____ minutes of screen time.

Today is another big day because you are going to remove social media from your phone. I know this is a bit scary, but don't worry, you can reinstall them tomorrow. You've been working so hard in the past week that I know you will be able to accomplish this significant milestone.

Now take your phone and uninstall all social media, including messaging apps. You can keep regular text and phone but turn off your notifications. The goal here is to have a social media cleanse, for 24 hours.

To be successful every time that you are mindlessly reaching for your phone to check social media, take a deep breath. Breathing in through the nose and breathing out through the mouth. Repeat until you feel calm and ready to get back to reality.

Today's screen-time result: _____ minutes

Day 18: Notifications Off

Today, I need to aim for _____ minutes of screen time.

YOU DID IT

You did a full 24 hours of social media cleanse!

BRAVO!

Now, that was probably the most significant test. If you failed, you could try again today (it's never too late).

If you succeeded, you deserve to reinstall your social media apps, but today, you will turn off all notifications, including your text notification. If you have dependents that might have to reach you in case of an emergency, tell them to call you if they need it.

Train yourself to check your phone every 3 hours. This exercise will be useful to regain control of your life and not always feel the need to look at your phone (statistics show that we pick up our phone 1500 times a week!). Catch yourself reaching for your device by mentally saying NO! Then redirect your attention toward the task you were doing.

Today's screen-time result: _____ minutes

Day 19: 2 Hours Only

Today, I need to aim for _____ minutes of screen time.

You are almost done your 21 days. Today's goal is to spend less than 2 hours of screen time, and if you can, no screen time at all. If you work in front of a screen, do the best to reduce screen time as much as possible. Screen time includes a TV or a computer screen.

How are you going to occupy your off-screen time today?

_____

_____

_____

Today's screen-time result: _____ minutes

Day 20: Leave Your Phone At Home

Today, I need to aim for _____ minutes of screen time.

Can you spend a day without your phone? Let's try to leave your smart technology at home. Like mentioned before, if someone has to reach out in case of an emergency, provide them with a work phone. You can also find a smart way, like giving them a friend's phone number or letting them know where you will be. There is always a way for people to reach you in case of emergency, having your phone on you 24/7 for emergencies is not a good excuse.

How did it feel to be technology free today?

_____

_____

_____

Would you do it again? If no, why? If yes, when?

_____

_____

_____

Today's screen-time result: _____ minutes

Day 21: Success

Today, I need to aim for _____ minutes of screen time.

YOU DID IT!

YOU'VE COMPLETED THE 21 DAYS TO UNPLUG. CONGRATULATIONS!

What have you learned so far?

_____

_____

_____

How can you implement what you've learned in your daily life? How can you maintain all the great progress you've accomplished so far?

_____

_____

_____

What offline way can you celebrate this success?

_____

_____

_____

Screen time when I started _____ minutes vs Screen time today _____ minutes.

CONCLUSION

Conclusion

Our digital world is an easy escape of reality, but it comes at a cost. As you have seen in previous chapters, the impact on our brain, physical body, and behaviors can be significant in one's life and ruin relationships with people we love.

Increasing our awareness of how we use technology is key to succeeding in adopting healthier behaviors and maintaining a balanced life. Not only are we more likely to change our habits, but we are also more likely to change our life by being in control of our screen time.

Our relationship with technology doesn't have to be non-existent, but we have to find a balance. Being in control means that use technology for your benefit, not the opposite. Don't let all your energy and time go to waste on browsing social media and entering a rabbit hole after looking at the weather on your phone.

As you experienced during the 21-day challenge, mindfulness and transferring your activities to be more offline than in front of the screen can improve your well-being. Being offline also increases your sense of living in the present moment. Experiencing your reality can be more rewarding than the digital world.

It is recommended to continue to monitor your screen time; awareness will be essential to maintain a healthy relationship with technology. Not only will you be able to regain a life that is fulfilling, and you will also set an excellent example for others to follow.

Nicky Dare's Living the Life Moments

Helpful Resources:

Book "Safety and Survival: Personal Preparedness Assessment Guide" (Exclusive Edition, 2019)

Book "The Audacity of Veracity" (2014)

Ebook "Dare To Unleash Greatness" (2018)

Ebook "Dare To Succeed In Life" (2018)

Book "Small Habits That Can Change Your Life" (2020)

For more inspirational resources from Nicky Dare, please visit:

Dare Blog: https://NickyDare.blogspot.com

Dare Vlog: https://youtube.com/c/NickyDare

Your feedback is a gift!

If you have reached to this page: thank you!

I would love to hear your thoughts, and feedback after you read this guide.

If you wish, please leave your review on the amazon page, or email us: books@nickydare.

com, or directly to me: hello@nickydare.com.

Thank you so very much in advance.

I hope you enjoy this easy-to-read guide to help you live the fulfilling life that you desire and deserve today.

XOXO,

Nicky Dare

About The Author

Educator, Author, Founder of iDARE® and DARE Education, President IAW International Association of Women of Santa Clarita Chapter, Corporate Consultant for Change Management and BPR Business Process Re-Engineering, Advocate for Disaster Preparedness, Safety and Survival, most importantly just a prolific human.

Nicky Dare is a seasoned multi-disciplinary professional with extensive experience in business development and strategic planning executive. Her success as a consultant and corporate coach has led her all around the world where she's transformed individuals and businesses alike. Ms. Dare's robust skillset is not merely limited to office settings. She's founded three, yes three, different organizations; Global Meta Management Consultants, Dare Education, and iDARE® Inc. The latter two focuses on personal development in the form of safety preparedness education. As a skilled marksman, Ms. Dare believes that knowledge surrounding emergency preparedness and firearm expertise is paramount. Her non-profit, iDARE® Inc., was born out of a vision from the most powerful mentor in her life; her father. He instilled the importance of living life filled with truth and purpose. Operating off these pillars, iDARE® Inc. is dedicated to helping development communities, empowering women, and educating children that have been impacted by disasters. It is apparent that Ms. Dare's "pillars of excellence" derived from her family values and strong academic and education background including her grandfather who was a prominent figure and reputable District Attorney in Indonesia.

Nicky Dare has a wide range of skills and a deep well of knowledge that she wishes to share with the world. Her book, The Audacity of Veracity, looks at how to create a life filled with health and happiness. This recent publication joins her webinar series on personal development, Safety and Survival: Personal Preparedness Assessment. She's also launched a podcast and does various speaking events, all as a means to share her powerful messages with as many people as possible. A passionate philanthropist, incredible personal life coach, and highly-effective corporate consultant, Ms. Dare truly makes a positive impact on the lives of everyone she meets by helping them to live with a purpose and passion.

She is proud to be a multilingual women's advocate, supporting her community on the committees of various charities and networking organizations. Dare's books and the startup of the iDARE® organization have been fully funded by her late father, who has been the ultimate mentor and inspiration in her life.

Her books are available on Amazon.

Printed in the United States
by Baker & Taylor

Printed in the United States
By Bookmasters